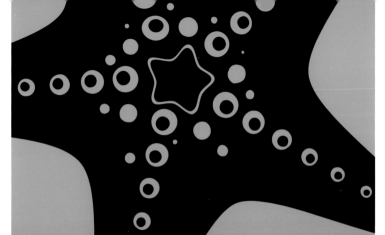

Can You Guess What I Am?

At the Seaside

JP Percy

W
FRANKLIN WATTS
LONDON • SYDNEY

How to use this book

The seaside is the place where the land and the sea meet. Not all seaside places look the same. The seaside can be a sandy beach, a rocky beach, cliffs or a man-made **harbour** – or all of these things!

This book combines the fun of a guessing game with some simple information about familiar things found at the seaside.

Start by guessing
- Carefully study the picture on the right-hand page.
- Decide what you think it might be, using both the picture and the clue.
- Turn the page and find out if you are right.

Don't stop there
- Read the extra information about the animal or object on the following page.
- Turn the page back – did you miss some interesting details?
- Have a go at the fun activities on page 22.

Enjoy guessing and learning
- Don't worry if your guess is wrong – this happens to everyone sometimes.
- Your guessing will get better the more you learn.

Words in **bold** can be found in the glossary on page 23.

I am made from thousands of grains of sand.

I am a sandy beach!

Sand is made by waves smashing rocks and shells into tiny grains. Waves wash the grains up onto the beach.

Sand dunes form when the wind and waves move the sand into large piles.

You make me with a bucket and spade.
Can you guess what I am?

I am a sandcastle!

Sandcastles are made from sand that is not too wet and not too dry.

Water helps the sand grains stick together, so the sandcastle won't fall down easily.

We are small and hard and come in lots of shapes and colours.
Can you guess what we are?

We are seashells!

Seashells are homes for animals such as **clams** and sea snails.

These animals are called **molluscs**. They have hard shells, which protect their soft bodies.

The sea fills me with water every day and I am a home for small sea animals. Can you guess what I am?

I am a rock pool!

When the tide comes in, the sea covers rocks and beaches along the seashore.

When the tide goes out, some of the seawater is trapped by rocks and forms a rock pool.

I also have a hard shell, but I have six legs and two claws that nip.
Can you guess what I am?

I am a crab!

Some crabs live in rock pools. Other crabs live in the sand or in the sea. They use their claws to grab and hold food or to fight other crabs.

I often wash up onto the beach and I am slimy to touch.
Can you guess what I am?

I am Seaweed!

Some seaweed has little bubbles full of air to help it float in the sea.

You can tell how high the tide was by where you find seaweed on the seashore.

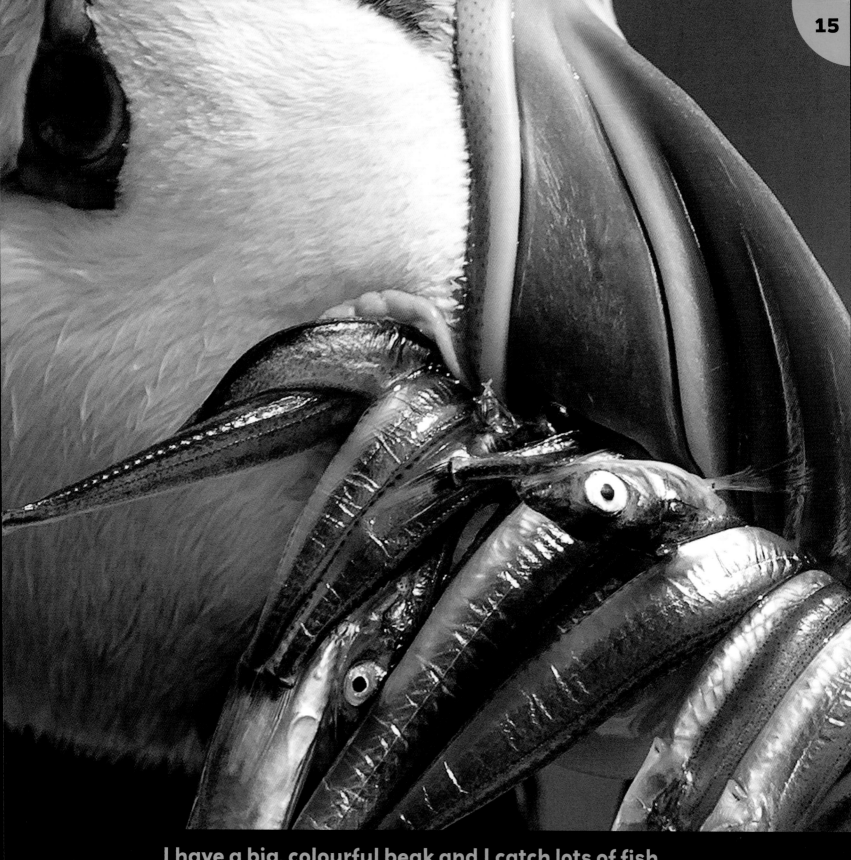

I have a big, colourful beak and I catch lots of fish.
Can you guess what I am?

I am a Puffin!

Puffins are seabirds that nest on cliffs.

Their colourful beaks can hold more than ten **sand eels** or other small fish at a time!

I am red and white with a bright light on top.
Can you guess what I am?

I am a lighthouse!

Lighthouses are put in places where there is a harbour or dangerous rocks or cliffs.

The bright light and red-and-white tower can be seen from far away by people on boats. This helps people on boats stay safe.

I am big and wet and I am the colour of the sky.

I am the sea!

A sea is a huge
area of salt water.

Water is see-through, but the sea sometimes
looks blue or grey. If the sky is blue the sea will look
blue. This is because the sea **reflects** the colour of the sky.

The wind blows the sea into waves.
Most waves are small but some are huge!

Now try this...

Guess it!

Can you guess what these three seaside objects are without the help of a picture?

1. I have five legs and I live in rock pools. Can you guess what I am?

2. I am cold and sweet and you eat me from a cone. Can you guess what I am?

3. I have sails and I float on water. Can you guess what I am?

(answers on page 23)

Spot it!

There are lots of things to see at the seaside. Draw a seaside picture that includes some of the items below. But watch out – there are three things that don't belong at the seaside. Can you spot the odd ones out?

- rock pool
- fishing boat
- starfish
- lighthouse
- seaweed
- spaceship
- seagull
- lion
- beach
- sea
- igloo
- crab

(answers on page 23)

Make it!

You don't need to visit the seaside to make a sandcastle. Mix some water with some sand until it starts to stick together. Pack the sand into a small bucket and tip it out onto a sand table, sandpit or a piece of stiff board. Decorate your sandcastle with pebbles, flags or shells.

Glossary

clam a type of mollusc. A clam has two shells that close around its body.

harbour a place where ships shelter from rough seas and bad weather.

mollusc an animal with no backbone and a soft body, such as a snail. Most molluscs have a shell.

reflect an image of something seen on a shiny surface, such as seeing your face in a mirror.

sand eel these animals are not eels, they are a different type of small fish. They burrow in the sand to stay safe from strong tides.

tide when the sea rises and falls. High tide is when the sea is closest to the land. Low tide is when the sea is furthest from the land.

Index

Spot it! answers
The odd ones out are:
spaceship, lion and igloo

Guess it! answers
1. a starfish
2. an ice cream
3. a sail boat

Franklin Watts
First published in Great Britain in 2016 by The Watts Publishing Group

Series editor: Amy Stephenson
Art director: Peter Scoulding
Picture Credits: John Braid/Dreamstime: 16. Marta Jonina/Shutterstock: front cover tc.
Rico K/Dreamstime: 18. Rico K/Shutterstock: 17.
Bas Meelker/Shutterstock: 4. Mark Metcalf/Shutterstock: 15.
Juan Moyano/Dreamstime: 5, 6. Oleandra/Shutterstock: front cover bl, 3.
Pix/Alamy: 9, 10. Maryna Pleshkun/Shutterstock: front cover tr, 7, 8.
Michael Sheehan/Dreamstime: 19, 20. Kirill Smalugov/Dreamstime: front cover cl, cr & bc.
Marzanna Syncerz/Dreamstime: 2, 22. Artur Synenko/Shutterstock: front cover br, 11, 12.
Verastuchelova/Dreamstime: 14. Zharate/Dreamstime: front cover tl, 13.

Dewey number: 577.699
ISBN: 978 1 4451 4474 0
Library eBook ISBN: 978 1 4451 4478 8

Printed in China

Franklin Watts
An imprint of
Hachette Children's Group
Part of The Watts Publishing Group
Carmelite House
50 Victoria Embankment
London EC4Y 0DZ

an Hachette UK company.
www.hachette.co.uk

www.franklinwatts.co.uk